bought in Egypt
Nov. 2014
Love Auntie S.

GIOVANNA MAGI

THE PYRAMIDS
OF GIZA AND THE SPHINX

BONECHI

THE GIZA PLATEAU

A - MORTUARY COMPLEX OF MENKAURE

1) Pyramid
2) Three "satellite" pyramids
3) Mortuary temple
4) Causeway
5) Valley temple

B - MORTUARY COMPLEX OF KHAFRE

1) Pyramid
2) "Satellite" pyramid
3) Mortuary temple and solar barks
4) Causeway
5) Valley temple

C - MORTUARY COMPLEX OF CHEOPS

1) Great Pyramid
2) Pyramids of the Queens and Bark Pits
3) Mortuary temple
4) Causeway

D - EASTERN NECROPOLIS

E - WESTERN NECROPOLIS

F - SPHINX

G - SPHINX TEMPLE

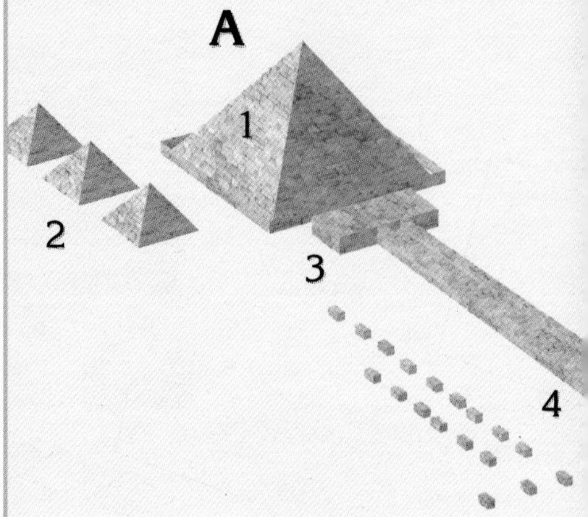

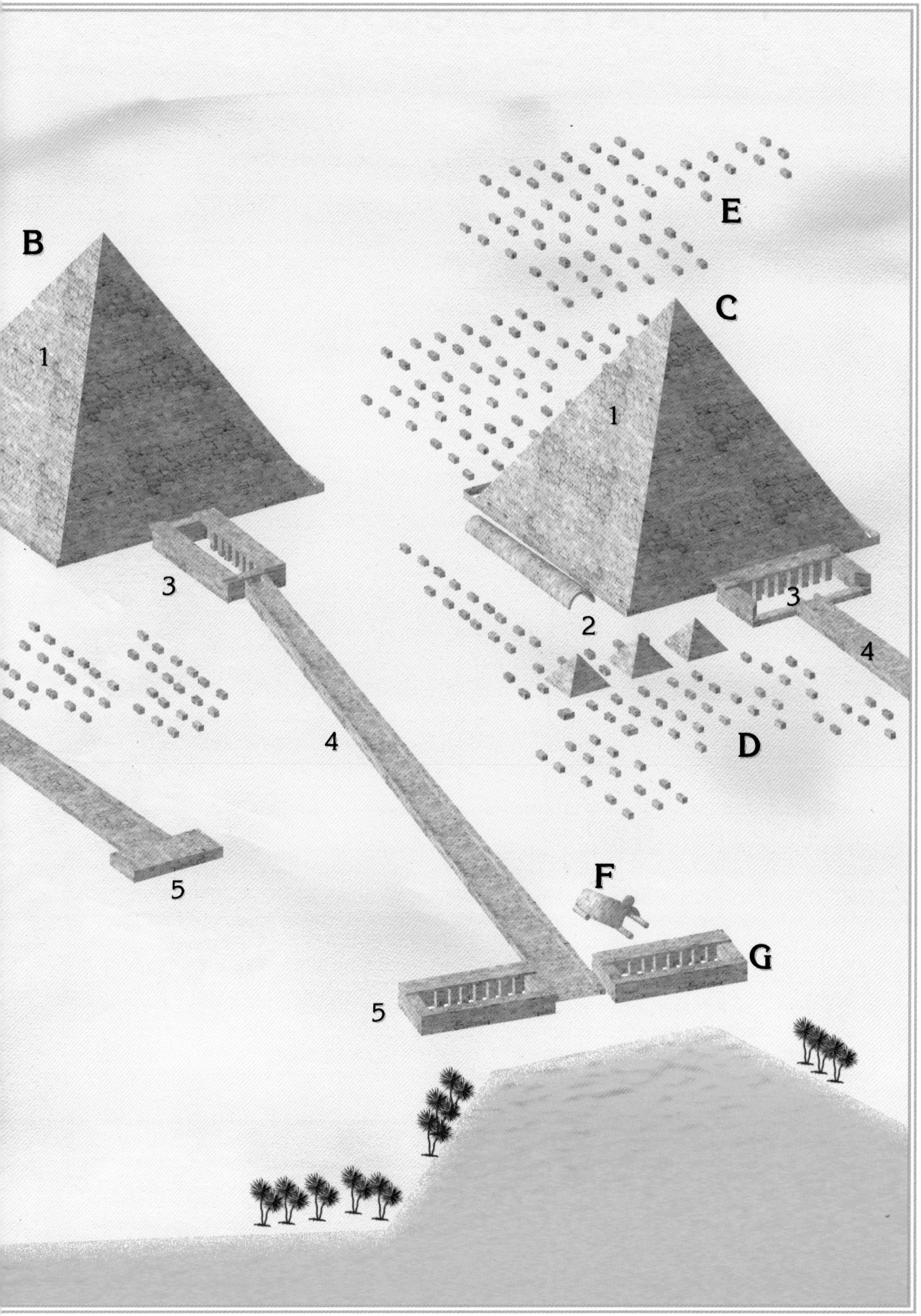
B
1
3
4
5
E
C
1
2
3
4
D
F
G
5

INTRODUCTION

Almost five thousand years ago, the Giza plateau, on the west bank of the Nile (the region of the dead), became the royal necropolis of Memphis, the capital of the pharaohs of the 4th Dynasty.
The Giza site lies about 9 miles (15 km) west of modern Cairo and covers an area of about 21.500 square feet (2000 m^2).
On the southwest side, a 130-foot (40 m) cliff descends to where there once ran a channel of the Nile, the borderline between the fertile land and the desert.
The Pyramids of Giza is the only one of the **Seven Wonders of the Ancient World** to have survived to our day; the others (the Pharos of Alexandria, the Colossus of Rhodes, the Mausoleum of Halicarnassus, the Temple of Artemis at Ephesus, the Statue of Zeus at Olympia, and the Hanging Gardens of Babylon) have long since disappeared, canceled out by the hand of men and by Time. The Giza site instead still hosts the tombs of three pharaohs of the 4th Dynasty – the pyramids of **Cheops** (Khufu), **Khafre** (or Chefren, Khefren), and **Menkaure** (or Mykerinus) – and the **Sphinx**, the "Father of Terror."
The intriguing appeal of these stones and the air of mystery that has emanated from them since ancient times has deeply stirred the minds and souls of scientists and archaeologists, writers and poets, painters and soldiers over the ages.
Not even Napoleon was immune to their seduction. On 21 July 1798, when his soldiers were about to engage in battle with the Mameluke army and arrayed before the uncertain geometry of the pyramids, **Napoleon** turned to them and, indicating the monuments, exclaimed, ***"Soldiers! From atop these pyramids, fifty centuries look down upon you!"***

Detail of the Battle of the Pyramids, *painted by Louis Lejeune (1775-1848) and today in the Château de Versailles.*

An Egyptian saying tells us that "All the world fears Time, but Time fears the Pyramids."

The pyramids are much more than the symbol of Egypt: they are a *déjà-vu* that each time surprises and perturbs; they are a challenge, a myth in stone, a staircase to eternity.

The word used by the ancient Egyptians for "pyramid" was mr, *but they also distinguished the three monuments at Giza by the names of Horizon of Cheops, Great is Khafre, and Divine is Menkaure. The etymology of the Greek term* piramis, *from which "pyramid" originates, is uncertain; it may, however, derive from the term* per-emaus *used by the ancient Egyptians to indicate the height of the monuments.*

General Features of the Pyramids

The three pyramids stand in relation to the four cardinal points along a diagonal axis from northeast to southwest, so that no one of the pyramids ever blocks the sun to the others. This perfect alignment has led to theories that the ancient Egyptians, experts in astronomical measurements as they were, took the positions of certain stars into consideration in their construction plans. According to the archaeologist Robert Bauval, the three large pyramids of Giza are actually meant to be in an alignment resembling that of the three "belt" stars in the constellation Orion. The pyramids are built mainly of limestone and granite – the first from the quarries of Tura, across the Nile from Memphis, and the second from Aswan. Unfortunately, in the13th century the Arabs began removing the precious casing stones from the limestone blocks and using them to build homes in Cairo. The pyramids are not isolated constructions: each is part of a funerary complex made up of a **mortuary temple** (or upper temple) to the east of the pyramid, a **causeway** – a sort of ceremonial route – and a **valley temple**. The valley temple symbolized the entry of the pharaoh into the world of the gods: it was in fact here that the sacred rite of the opening of the mouth began. The valley temple of Cheops has been almost completely destroyed, but a large part portion of that of Khafre is well preserved. The funeral procession traveled the causeway to the mortuary temple and the pyramid, carrying the dead pharaoh on the sacred bark toward his place of eternal rest. In the mortuary temple, the pharaoh became a divinity and as such was adored. A common feature of all three pyramids is the **burial chamber**, almost exactly aligned with the center axis of the construction. The main pyramids of Menkaure and Cheops are each flanked by three satellite pyramids, while that of Khafre has only one.

". . . They built a stairway to the sky so that I might reach the sky on it . . . the sky made the rays of the Sun solid so that I might raise myself up to the eyes of Ra . . ."

It is said that Napoleon, on his journey to Egypt, had calculated that with the blocks of stone used in the construction of the Giza pyramid complex it would have been possible to erect a wall around France about 13 feet (almost 4 m) in height and about one foot (30 cm) thick.
It also seems that the emperor's rule-of-thumb calculation was confirmed by the mathematicians in his retinue.

The Pyramids in Numbers

Pyramid of Cheops

4th Dynasty
2590 - 2565 BC

Original height: 480.9 ft (146.60 m)
Actual height: 455.2 ft (138.75 m)
Side: 755.8 ft (230.37 m)
Inclination: 51° 50’

Pyramid of Khafre

4th Dynasty
2558 - 2533 BC

Original height: 470.8 ft (143.50 m)
Actual height: 447.5 ft (136.40 m)
Side: 706 ft (215.20 m)
Inclination: 53° 10’

Pyramid of Menkaure

4th Dynasty
2532 - 2515 BC

Height: 216.5 ft (66 m)
Side: 341.2 ft (104 m)
Inclination: 51° 20’

THE GREAT PYRAMID OF CHEOPS:
A TECHNOLOGICAL MIRACLE, AN ENIGMA IN STONE

The Great Pyramid, which the ancient Egyptians called the Horizon of Cheops, was built 45 centuries ago and is the largest at Giza. Our notions of its history come mainly from the historian and "journalist" Herodotus, who visited Egypt in 460-455 BC. He tells us that the pyramid was "twenty years in the making" and its builders and those of the causeway "worked in gangs of a hundred thousand men, each gang for three months." He also relates how an inscription reports that 1,600 silver talents were spent on radishes, onions, and garlic for the workmen. We must, of course, remember that Herodotus saw the pyramids 2700 years after their completion and by his own admission was in many cases only repeating hearsay. The estimates by today's archaeologists of the number of workers range between fifteen and twenty thousand workers. The architect was apparently a certain Hemiunu, who in building his creation used about 2,300,000 blocks of limestone averaging about 2.5 tons each, for a total weight of aproximately 6,000,000 tons! The outer facing is no longer, since beginning in the 13th century the beautiful slabs of limestone were removed for reuse in building the homes and the mosques of the new city of Cairo, thus exposing the gigantic structural blocks underneath.

WHO WAS CHEOPS?

The name of Cheops, the second king of the 4th Dynasty, is the derived Greek form of the ancient Egyptian Khufu, meaning “He [the god] Protects Me.”
We know very little of this pharaoh; likewise, few images have come down to us. Paradoxically, all that remains of the builder of the world’s largest pyramid is a tiny ivory statuette, just 2.76 inches (7 cm) high, bearing the features of the man Herodotus described as an evil, cruel ruler who even went so far as to sell his daughter into prostitution to obtain financing for construction of his monument.

Ivory statuette of Cheops. Cairo, Egyptian Museum.

At the top of the Great Pyramid is a flat terrace about 33 feet (10 m) square, where the pyramidion or capstone originally stood. A large block of limestone found near one of the satellite pyramids has recently been identified as its base. The reconstructed pyramidion alongside the Great Pyramid may have served as a maquette (a preliminary model) for the architect. The Great Pyramid squares the circle: the perimeter of its square base is the same length as the circumference of a circle with a radius equal to its height.

Inside the Great Pyramid

1 - Entrance to the pyramid at 82 ft (25 m) above ground level, on the north face.

2 - Down-sloping corridor leading to the subterranean chamber.

3 - Subterranean chamber (original burial chamber), at 98.4 ft (30 m) below ground level.

4 - Descending passage, probably used to permit the workers to exit the pyramid after the King's Chamber had been sealed.

5 - Ascending passage, a little over 3 ft (1 m) in height, leading to the Queen's Chamber.

6 - The Queen's Chamber or middle chamber, lying exactly on the axis of the pyramid.

7 - The Grand Gallery, the architectural masterpiece of ancient Egypt. It is 154.2 ft (47 m) long and 26.25 ft (8 m) high, with a ceiling formed of a massive blocks fitted together with uncanny precision.

8 - Three red granite "plugs" that slid vertically to hermetically seal the sarcophagus chamber.

9 - The sarcophagus chamber or King's Chamber, 19.2 ft (5.85 m) in height, 34.3 ft (10.45 m) long and 17.1 ft (5.22 m) wide, at 157.5 ft (48 m) from ground level, completely faced in blocks of pink granite. The ceiling is composed of nine slabs each weighing over 400 tons. On the west side of the chamber is the red granite sarcophagus of the king, with no cover and no inscriptions. It is 7.34 ft (2.24 m) long and 3.38 ft (1.03 m) high. Nothing was found inside it – neither mummy nor ornaments.

10 - The so-called "construction chambers," a system of five small, empty compartments, one above the other and extremely low-ceilinged, the top one with a double-sloping roof. The first of these chambers was discovered by Nathaniel Davison in 1765, the others by Perring and Vyse in 1837. They were thought to be primarily designed to relieve the enormous pressure exerted by the overlying mass of the pyramid on the ceiling of the King's Chamber. The name "Khufu" was discovered, daubed in red paint, on some

Two engravings by Luigi Mayer (1804) of the passage uniting the second and the third galleries (above) and of the sarcophagus chamber (below). Paris, Bibliothèque des Arts Décoratifs.

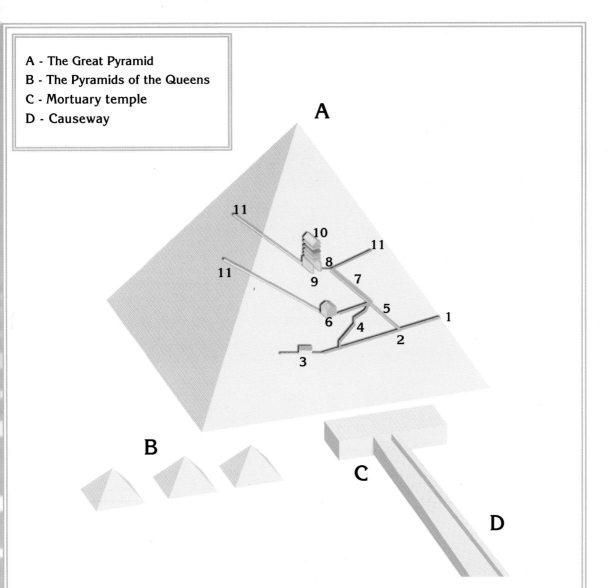

A - The Great Pyramid
B - The Pyramids of the Queens
C - Mortuary temple
D - Causeway

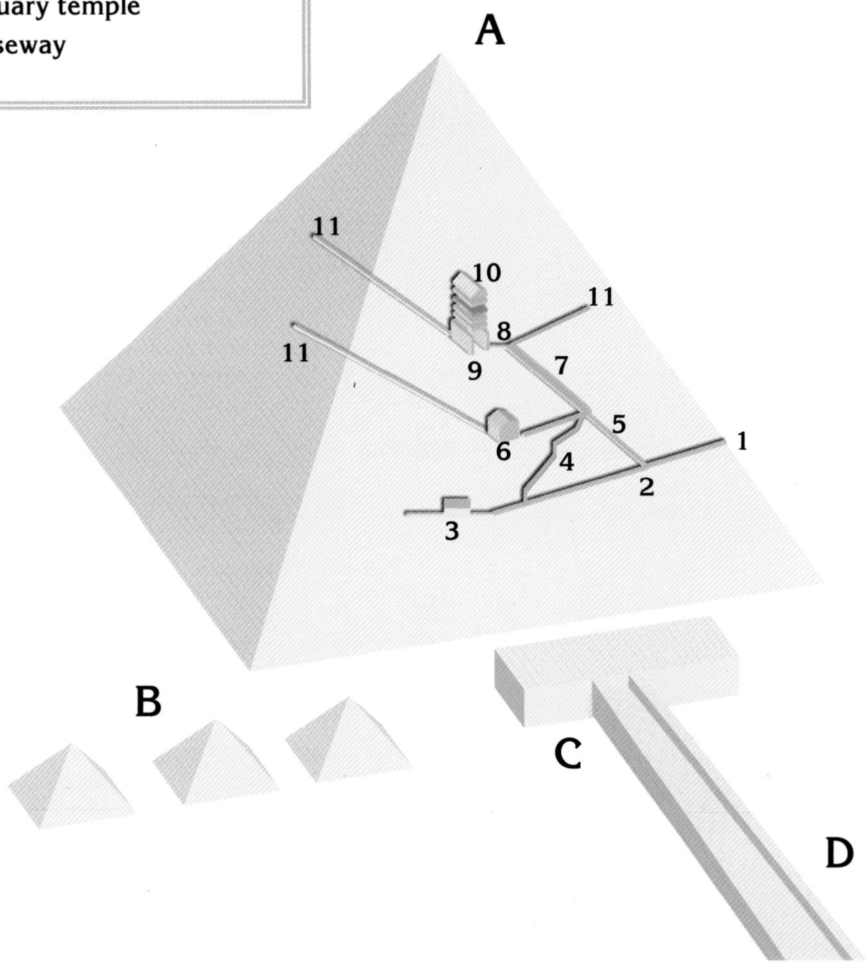

The Grand Gallery.

The entrance to the sarcophagus chamber.

of the walls and ceilings of this curious internal monument. In section, this tower is strangely reminiscent of the *Zed*, or backbone of Osiris.

11 - Ventilation shafts. These two ducts, which open at a height of 249.4 ft (76 m) on the north and south faces of the pyramid, carry air to the burial chamber.

Napoleon's Secret

Napoleon Bonaparte was one of the many visitors who have ventured inside the Great Pyramid. He did so on 12 August 1799; the chronicles of the time recount that when he emerged, he was visibly shaken and refused to speak of his experience to anyone. It is said that even much later, as he lay on his deathbed on Saint Helena, all Napoleon would say to his faithful valet who insisted on knowing what had happened was that it was useless to tell, "since no one would believe it anyway."

Cheops and the Stars

The fifth-century philosopher Proclus of Byzantium stated that the Great Gallery of Cheops' pyramid was originally an **astronomical observatory** that the pharaoh only later used as his tomb. This view was shared by a number of 18th-century astronomers.
In any event, scholars have demonstrated that at the time of construction of the pyramids the two ventilation shafts of the Royal Chamber, which communicate with the outside, were aligned with the stars of the ancient sky: the north shaft with the circumpolar stars, in particular Thuban, and the south shaft with Orion's belt.

The construction and purpose of the pyramid have been explained in the most disparate manners: an astronomical observatory, a magical temple, a work by aliens or the people of the fabled Atlantis. And many others . . . but when all is said and done, the pyramid remains. It is a magnificent transposition of the sun's rays into stone, and today we – with all our sophisticated technology – can only continue to ask ourselves how was it ever possible to transport two and a half million blocks of stone to such heights in an age when the wheel, the pulley, and the winch were unknown.

The Pyramids of the Queens

The three monuments called the Pyramids of the Queens are located to the eastern side of the Great Pyramid of Cheops. Like the Great Pyramid, they were built of blocks of limestone and covered with a casing. They all have an inclination of 52° and a simple corridor giving access to the rock-hewn burial chamber. Standing before the eastern face of each was a mortuary temple similar to that of Cheops.
Tradition has it that the southernmost pyramid belonged to **Queen Henutsen**, Cheops' wife and half-sister – and mother of Khafre. The middle pyramid is attributed to **Queen Merityetes**, mother of Djedefre (Radjedef), and the last to **Queen Hetepheres**, wife of Snefru and mother of Cheops.
During the reign of the Psusennes I, a pharaoh of the 21st Dynasty, the mortuary temple of the pyramid of Henutsen was transformed into a chapel dedicated to the cult of Isis, the "Lady of the Pyramids."
Despite the legends, the attribution of the three small pyramids to the three queens is supported only by one inscription found in this chapel; we must therefore at least consider the hypothesis that the three monuments may have had another purpose. A Polish scholar has advanced the fascinating theory that these pyramids were **models**, in about 1:5 scale, of the Great Pyramid, erected by the architects during the course of work on the principal monument; we know for a fact that its plan underwent major changes and modifications during construction.
And it is, of course, possible that once the Great Pyramid was completed, these three scale models were in fact used as tombs for the three queens.

A Queen and Her Treasure

On 2 February 1925, a few dozen meters from the pyramid of Cheops, a photographer with the archaeological expedition financed by the Harvard Fine Arts Museum of Boston tripped while carrying his tripod and thus discovered the opening of a shaft about 98.5 feet (30 m) deep. The archeologist of the expedition, the American George Reisner, took two years to empty this shaft tomb, which turned out to be not the original burial place but the site of the re-entombment of Hetepheres, wife of Snefru and mother of Cheops.
Amassed haphazardly inside the tomb were the queen's grave goods, the most complete and best preserved of the Old Kingdom funerary treasures, today at the Egyptian Museum of Cairo.
One of the pieces found in the tomb is a bed in wood and gold leaf, the same materials used for a chair, the arms of which reproduce an elegant motif of three lotus flowers. Inside the chests and coffers were found toilet objects like implements for nail care, containers for cosmetics, and jars for perfumed oils and unguents. There is also a collection of twenty silver bracelets with delicate butterfly-motif inlays in cornelian, lapis-lazuli, and turquoise.

Hetepheres' chair in wood and gold leaf, 31.5 in (80 cm) high and 28 in (71 cm) wide. Cairo, Egyptian Museum.

THE PYRAMID OF KHAFRE

The measurements of this pyramid are slightly inferior to those of Cheops', but Khafre built slightly higher up the slight slope of the plateau so as to give the impression that his mortuary monument was actually taller than that built by his father.
Originally 470.8 feet (143.50 m) in height, the pyramid now measures 447.5 feet (136.40 m), with 706-foot (215 m) sides. Of the three pyramids of Giza, this is the only one to have preserved some of its original Tura limestone facing on its topmost part.
For a long time it was thought that Khafre's construction was solid, with no internal burial chambers, but in 1818 the Italian archaeologist **Giovanni Battista Belzoni** noticed an unusual accumulation of detritus on the north side of the pyramid, and ". . . after thirty days' work, I had the satisfaction of entering the interior of a pyramid that had always been believed impenetrable."
In the central chamber he found no treasure, but only a pink granite sarcophagus "buried almost level with the floor."
Belzoni's lampblack boast "Scoperto da G. Belzoni, 2 marzo 1818" is still visible on the wall. But Belzoni better than any other knew that he was not the first "discoverer" and that the pyramid had been opened and then resealed long before his time, probably in about 1200. He in fact found a number of phrases written in charcoal on the wall, in Arabic script; one of these read, "Mohammed Ahmed, quarryman, opened this with the assistance of Othman and the consent of king Ali Mohammed, from the beginning to the end."

Who was Khafre?

Khafre, son of Cheops and Queen Henutsen, ascended the throne of Egypt after the early death of his older brother Djedefre, Cheops' direct successor. He reigned, it would seem, for twenty-five or twenty-six years, even though Manethon erroneously attributed him a reign of sixty-six years. Of this pharaoh, whose coronation name means "Ra Elevates Him," there has come down to us a diorite statue found by Mariette in 1860 in Khafre's valley temple. This statue, considered one of the highest artistic expressions of ancient Egypt, shows the young pharaoh, with a young, muscular body, his face infused with an absolute, supernatural serenity, seated on a throne; clinging to the back of his neck is the spread-winged falcon god Horus, embracing the nemes of the pharaoh in a gesture of divine protection.

The diorite statue of Khafre is 5.5 feet (1.68 m) tall; the sides of the throne are decorated with bas-reliefs of the sema tauy*; that is, the union of Upper and Lower Egypt symbolized by the emblematic plants of the regions, the lotus and the papyrus.*

THE MORTUARY COMPLEX OF KHAFRE

In front of the east face of the pyramid was the **mortuary temple of Khafre**. Unfortunately, today there remain only a few traces of the structure, among which a block of granite weighing more than 400 tons.

The facade of the temple must have been about 361 feet (110 m) in length, with a large vestibule with 14 columns and a vast rectangular hall (also columned) opening on a broad porticoed courtyard.

The pits containing the solar barks of the pharaoh were dug on the north and south sides.

A causeway, 540 yards (494 m) long, united this temple to the **valley temple** discovered by Mariette in 1852 and which has reached us come down to us in good condition.

The valley temple is a solemn, austere edifice of large blocks of pink Aswan granite; the large great hall, in the form of an inverted T, was supported by sixteen monolithic pillars each 13.6 feet (4.15 m) high. Along the walls there originally stood twenty-three diorite and alabaster statues of the pharaoh, which have all disappeared save for that found by Mariette and today on display at the Egyptian Museum of Cairo.

Three views of the valley temple of Khafre: the excellent state of preservation of the structure permits observing the absolute precision with which the blocks of granite were joined.

THE PYRAMID OF MENKAURE

The pyramid of Menkaure is just 216.5 feet (66 m) high and 341.2 feet (104 m) per side. In 1500 it still boasted its beautiful exterior facing, which later in history was almost completely removed. The lower part of the pyramid is made of blocks of red Aswan granite (much of which is still in place), which contrasted with the upper portion in white Tura limestone. Herodotus described the pyramid as being "... covered for half its height in Ethiopian stone."

The entrance to the pyramid, on the north face at about 13 feet (4 m) above ground level, was found on 29 July 1837 by the Englishmen Richard William Vyse and John Shea Perring. Menkaure's burial chamber is complexly structured, unlike those of Cheops and Khafre; this fact reflects a series of transformations that could only have been made during the course of work. There are thus two burial chambers, one original and one newer, lower, and final.

In the latter, Vyse discovered a basalt sarcophagus decorated with the typical "palace facade" reliefs, with its cover broken, containing a wooden sarcophagus and the remains of a mummified body.

Unfortunately, both the beautiful sarcophagus and what might have been the remains of Menkaure were lost in 1838 when the *Beatrice* sank off Carthage as she was carrying them to England.

Who was Menkaure?

Menkaure succeeded his father Khafre and was the next-to-last pharaoh of the 4th Dynasty. Although Manethon tells us that this "just and pious pharaoh" reigned sixty-three years, he actually occupied the throne for a little less than thirty.
Menkaure was responsible for the construction of the third pyramid in the Giza complex, the smallest – but also the only one to still possess its three satellite pyramids.

Detail of the alabaster statue of Menkaure in the Egyptian Museum of Cairo.

An Old Kingdom text describes how the pharaoh was heading ". . . toward the plateau of the pyramids to observe the works done on the pyramid that is called Menkaure is Divine."

Due to the unique color contrast on its exterior, Menkaure's pyramid was called the "Painted Pyramid" by the Arabs.

Facing page, the final burial chamber, in which was found the sarcophagus of the pharaoh, and the descending passage leading to the burial chamber inside the pyramid of Menkaure.

The interior of the pyramid is quite complex. The original design called for a descending corridor from the base of the smaller original pyramid to the burial chamber; this approach was at some time abandoned, and another entrance was opened on the north side. This leads through an antechamber, the walls of which are decorated with bas-reliefs of the "palace facade" motif, to the burial chamber as originally planned. The plans were, however, again modified: underneath the original burial chamber another, much larger room was excavated (21.3 by 7.5 ft – 6.50 by 2.30 m, with a 13-foot – 4-meter – ceiling) and was faced in granite.

The Mortuary Temple of Menkaure

Unfortunately, very little remains of the mortuary temple begun by Menkaure in stone and completed in mudbrick by his son and successor Shepseskaf, although it was still intact in 1700. Some of the blocks used in its construction weigh as much as 200 tons. The temple stands on the west side of the pyramid. Its structure was quite complex, with a vestibule, a rectangular courtyard, a double-colonnaded portico that led to the sanctuary, and many annexes.
A sloping causeway united the mortuary temple with the **valley temple**, where the archaeologist George Reisner discovered, during excavations conducted in 1907 and 1908, the famous **schist triads** in which the pharaoh is associated with Hathor and other deities symbolizing as many Egyptian nomes.

Triad of Menkaure (Cairo, Egyptian Museum). To the pharaoh's right stands Hathor; to his left a female figure symbolic of the nome of Diospolis Parva.

The Satellite Pyramids

The three satellite pyramids, the largest smooth-sided and the other two stepped, rise to the south of the main pyramid of Menkaure. Each was in turn flanked, again to the south, by a small mortuary temple, in mudbrick with wooden columns.
Even though no proof has yet come to light, it is thought that the satellites belong to the royal brides of Menkaure. Two are unknown, but the third is Khamerernebti II, whose features are those of Hathor in the triads.
The measurements of the bases are one-third those of the main pyramid. Inside one of the satellites, Richard Vyse found the name of the pharaoh written in red ink.

THE GREAT SPHINX

An integral, and very famous, part of Khafre's funeral complex is the Great Sphinx, the gigantic crouching lion with a human countenance that many believe reproduces the facial features of the pharaoh.
The Sphinx, located southeast of the Great Pyramid of Cheops, is 76.4 feet (20 m) tall and 187 feet (57 m) long; the head, wearing the typical nemes, is 19.7 feet (6m) high.
The monument was modeled 4500 years ago from a natural knoll of limestone at Giza, containing rock of three different types.
Over the centuries, the blowing sand and wind have disfigured the powerful body and the enigmatic face.
To legitimize his ascent to the throne, the 18th Dynasty pharaoh Thutmose IV recounted how the Sphinx appeared to him in a dream and asked him to dig out the sand that covered it almost completely: "Thutmose, my son, I am your father Khepri-Ra-Atum; if you free me from the sand that oppresses me I will make you king and you will wear on your head the White Crown and the Red Crown."
Thutmose did as he was told, and also built retaining walls to halt the advance of the sand. To recall the event, he placed a pink granite stele, about 13 feet (4m) in height, between the paws of the Sphinx.

The Greek term "sphinx" derives from the ancient Egyptian *sheps-ankh* (the living image). In the New Kingdom, the Great Sphinx was associated with Harmakis (Horus at the Horizon); for the Arabs it was Abu el-Hol, the "Father of Terror."

In its extraordinary monumentality and mystery, the Sphinx, "half mountain and half crouching beast" (as it was defined by Pierre Loti), is a sculpture unique in all of Egyptian art.

David Roberts' rendering of a sandstorm approaching a caravan in front of the Great Sphinx. The scene is utter invention, since the Sphinx faces due east and therefore could never have the sun to its right.

A beautiful painting by Jean Léon Gérôme (1824-1904), in Cairo's Club des Diplomates, of General Napoleon Bonaparte and the Sphinx.

The Sphinx Temple

In front of the Sphinx, slightly to the right, are the remains of a small temple in limestone and pink Aswan granite, with two entrances.
It once boasted a courtyard with an interior colonnade of large rectangular pillars and an altar for offerings at the center. Its structure is similar to that of the valley temple of Khafre, which stands alongside it.
This temple may have been used for ceremonies on occasion of the jubilee of the pharaoh - or it might actually have been dedicated to the Great Sphinx. Unfortunately, in the temple itself there is no trace of decorative detail and no texts have yet provided us with any information about it.

An evocative view of the Sphinx through the doorways of the Khefren's valley temple.

The Solar Boat Museum

In May of 1954, the young archaeologist Kamal el-Mallak brought to light, on the southern side of the pyramid of Cheops, two huge rock-hewn pits closed by 41 enormous blocks of limestone, bearing the cartouches of Djedefre, the son and successor of Cheops. Inside the northern trench was found a wooden vessel that had been buried there after having been disassembled into 1224 pieces; it took more than ten years of painstaking work for the archaeologists to put the gigantic three-dimensional "jigsaw puzzle" together. Once reconstructed, the bark was placed on exhibit in the museum built especially for it near the pit in which it was found.

The **vessel**, built of cedar, sycamore, and jujube wood, is 150.9 feet (46 m) long and 19.7 feet (6 m) at the beam. Its slender form terminates at the prow and stern with mizen masts in the form of papyrus stems. At the center is a closed cabin, 29.5 feet (9 m) in length.

The bark was equipped with six pairs of oars, from 19.7 to 27.9 feet (6 to 8.5 m) length.

All the wooden elements were held together by ropes and pegs; no nails were used.

The second pit has yet to be opened, but a probe has revealed it to contain a bark similar to that reassembled from the pieces found in the first pit.

The significance of this bark has long been the subject of debate and discussion. The pit also contained ropes, and the vessel displays marks left by the ropes in its wood; these facts have led to conjecture that the bark was actually used on water. It may have been one of the vessels used by the pharaoh during his reign, or it may even be the bark on which the body of Cheops was transported along the causeway toward his eternal resting-place. It may also have a purely religious significance, as the **solar bark** on which the soul of the dead pharaoh journeyed to join the sun god Ra in his eternal celestial navigation.

Two views of the solar bark of Cheops, with its soaring papyrus prow and the central cabin.

THE PRIVATE CEMETERIES AT THE PYRAMID OF CHEOPS

East and west of the Great Pyramid are the two large private cemeteries of the highly-placed court officials and other personalities at the court of Cheops who had themselves buried alongside the tomb of their king in order to remain at his side even in death.
The two cemeteries, known as the **Eastern Necropolis** and the **Western Necropolis**, are made up of mastabas, aligned in two parallel rows and displaying many features in common: a stela-false door, an offerings room, and a burial chamber. Certain of these mastabas also contained the sculptures known as "**substitute heads**" in niches alongside the burial chamber. These sculptures represent only the head of the dead person, most certainly had a ritual function, and were characteristic only of the Old Kingdom.

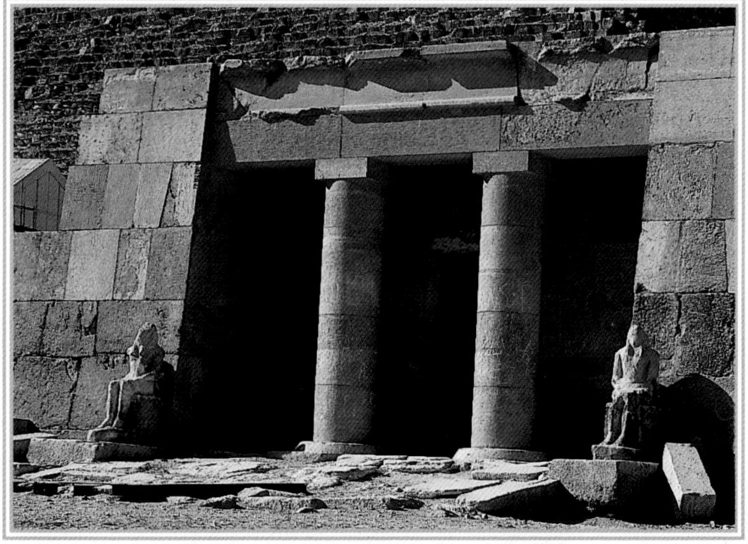

Above, the entrance of a 5th Dynasty mastaba.

Left, the entrance of the mastaba of Seshemnufer IV, Inspector of the Phisicians of the Grand House, late 5th Dynasty - 6 Dynasty.

Eastern Necropolis

To the east of the three secondary or satellite pyramids of the Great Pyramid of Cheops are the mastabas of court dignitaries and important figures in the pharaoh's retinue: the royal brides and, at their sides, the firstborn children followed by the others.
The **mastaba of Kufu-Kaef**, son of Cheops and Queen Henutsen, is decorated with beautiful bas-reliefs; although they have lost their original colors, they are otherwise in a state of perfect preservation.
Not far away are **mastabas of Qar** (or Mery-Nefer), a court official at the time of Pepys II (6th Dynasty), and of his son **Idou**. In both these tombs were found beautiful statues of the dead with their families.
On the opposite corner of the necropolis is the extraordinary **mastaba of Meresankh III**, the royal bride of Khafre. This tomb, which has for the most part retained its colored paintings, contains – at the back of a wide niche – ten large statues of Meresankh, the pharaoh's mother Hetepheres, his daughter Shepseskau, and other women of the family. Nearby is the large **mastaba of Prince Ankh-haf**.

Two views of the mastaba of Idu, a high court dignitary of the 4th Dynasty. Top, a detail of the false door with seated statue of the deceased receiving offerings. Bottom, statues of Idu set in niches.

Western Necropolis

The mastabas of the Western necropolis date to the 4th and 6th Dynasties.
Iasen, Inspector of Priests, embellished the walls of his tomb with painting illustrating scenes of rural life and of fishing.
The mastaba of **Kaemankh, Superintendent of the Treasury**, is also richly decorated.
The mastaba of **Imery, the Prophet of Cheops**, contains some of the most beautiful and best-preserved bas-reliefs to be found in the necropolis.

Mastaba of Qar. The statues of the deceased sculpted in the southern wall of the first chamber.

The Tombs of the Pyramid Builders

The hundreds upon hundreds of masons, stone-cutters, and stone-dressers who worked on construction of the three pyramids were also given their private necropolis.
About one kilometer west of Giza there have recently come to light the remains of about six hundred tombs, both large and small. Built mainly of mudbrick, and mostly pyramidal in form, these burial places, like their more important neighbors, are decorated with bas-reliefs and have been found to contain statues, crockery for cooking food, and inscriptions that tell us the titles of their occupants: "Inspector of Builders," "Superintendent of the Workers," etc.
The discovery of this necropolis is important for two reasons. First of all, because it finally overthrows Herodotus' theory regarding the construction of the pyramids with its attendant image of slaves forced to work for the glory of the pharaoh under the lash and in inhuman conditions: quite the contrary, the pyramid-builders were not slaves but free Egyptian citizens who received regular wages. Secondly, the decorations offer us an interesting glimpse of the daily lives of the workers who were permitted by the pharaoh to build their tombs so near the royal sepulchers.

How Were the Pyramids Built?

The debate over the system of construction used to raise the pyramids has consumed rivers of ink. Architects, engineers, archaeologists, and scholars of every persuasion have expressed their ideas in merit and made their contribution to finding a solution to one of the greatest unsolved mysteries of ancient Egypt.
Unfortunately, the copious iconography regarding daily life in ancient Egypt is not matched by a similar store of documentation of the construction of the most important monuments of Egyptian architecture.
Most certainly, the stone was quarried, cut into blocks, loaded onto sleds, runners, or rollers, and dragged to the pyramid construction site.
Once there, however, there arose the problem of how to lift these gigantic stones. The most highly-credited theory is by now that involving **ramps**: wide inclined planes, built of mudbrick or sand, that gradually increased in slope and height as the pyramid went up. The ramp may have been **straight** and perpendicular to the pyramid, built up to one side of it and becoming narrower at the top and longer as the pyramid grew in height. Or the ramp may have been **helicoidal**, spiraling around the structure.
Herodotus wrote, apropos of how a pyramid was built, "[It] was made after the manner of steps . . . and when they had first made it thus, they raised the remaining stones with machines made of short pieces of timber, raising them first from the ground to the first stage of the steps, and when the stone got up to this it was placed upon another machine standing on the first stage, and so from this it was drawn to the second upon another machine; for as many as were the courses of the steps, so many machines there were also . . ." The "machine" mentioned by Herodotus may be an ancestor of the modern-day crane, the operating principle of which reflects that of the *shaduf*, the counterpoised sweep still used in Egypt for irrigation purposes.

Ideal recontruction of the pyramid building site.

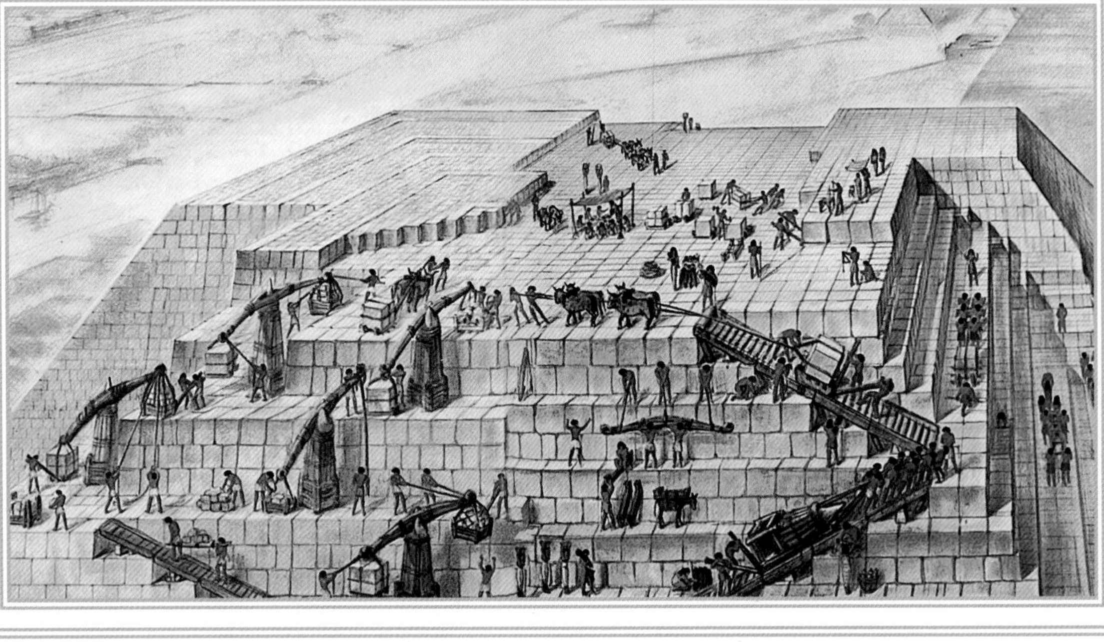